NOTHING REMEMBERS

poems by

MICHAEL DICKEL

Finishing Line Press
Georgetown, Kentucky

NOTHING REMEMBERS

Publisher: Leah Maines

Editor: Christen Kincaid

Cover Art: *ANGEL OF TIME* Oil Painting by Lica Kerenskaya (owned by
Michael Dickel). Image used by permission. ©2018

Author Photo: Zaki Qutteineh

Cover Design: Elizabeth Maines McCleavy

Printed in the USA on acid-free paper.
Order online: www.finishinglinepress.com
also available on amazon.com

Author inquiries and mail orders:
Finishing Line Press
P. O. Box 1626
Georgetown, Kentucky 40324
U. S. A.

Table of Contents

Life is transitory
and memory travels
its own twisted paths

I dedicate these poems to those
who travel the paths of our memories
and to those of us who re-member them

My love goes to
Aviva
Jules, Rhys, and Jett
Moshe, Sylvia, and Naomi

Land / 'scape / memory

RETURN FROM POMPEII

i
I write this from storm clouds
tumbling over a mountain
like ghostly echoes of its
famous volcanic eruption.
I saw them whip by
the train's window
and decided to ride
them, slipping out of
the passenger car unnoticed
just when you stopped my heart.
The rain of sound would form
meaning with lightning and thunder
if I had not fallen under the spell

of this place that is not formed.

ii
           Ashes fell down
from the sky, cinders, molten rock.
The living lay, buried there. Their
corpses eventually dried out, ashes
to ashes and dust to dust transcribed
literally, without translation. In a millennium
and a half, a little longer, the empty spaces
left behind become molds, the dead
become casts of cement.

So it is with the dead.

iii

                    The memories
of living fall around the lives
once lived, leave a hole in the
pumice. The emptiness fills with words—
narrative and song. That is why I write
with rain drops on your windows
as the train speeds by the valleys
indifferently. That is why the ghosts
do not speak to me or to you.
That is why no one noticed

as I left the train again.

FOLLOWING

Crumbling bread burnt,
charred before Pesach, and
pocketed bread bits dumped,
washed away to Rosh Hashanah.
Take me back to fields,
wheat grown and golden
waiting to be gathered in.
Take me back to loaves
raised from the earth,
shared sustainability,
quiet sustenance.

Woven loaf, a path
of possibility, blessed with
tastes, salted with tears,
sacrificed at the Temple
of remembrance and forgetting.
Take me back to ovens
hot in the kitchen,
the scent of new bread.
Take me back to yeast,
rising dough in a bowl,
and small hands helping.

Unraveling trails left
behind—bird-eaten during
hikes through stony hills—
above the desert heat,
below sky waters—
take me back to time,
swept forward and back
into revelations of you—
take me back to bread,
a beginning with an end,
a bite to eat, water to drink.

BLUE NOTES

Been there:

dusk-blue
Michigan shore,

seek-wind
night,

high-pitched;
siren-wail

sax whispers against
the breeze:

real-live
city, Chicago.

ANOTHER SUNSET PHOTO

Why do we love the sunset
so? Dark blood spills into
night—drunk fear stares into
a fire burning desire. Lovely
opening.
          But why do we love?
The sun setting so, repeated—
although only now, it seems,
this.

          Lovely. Like when you.
Before me. And I. With you.
Run like colors—
          into night.

          A flight of cranes
trumpets. A bit of reflection
drops into the dark,
which will not watch
the sun rise—that dark
which clouds sky.

          Mind.
Sleepless. Restless.
So the sunset enters
art, words, photos—
eyes us. Relentless,
unwilling to leave.
A radical end.

AMBITIONS / DISCONNECT / TRUTH

I do not have ambitions to be
the one here who will soar
from bridges to rivers and back.
Even when I am tempted to drift
in the sweet air between here and then
I don't have ambitions to be
the one here who will soar.

Severed phone cords disconnect
the conversation we never could start
from bridges to rivers and back.
Over even drifts of snow, in the moment
between single signal pulses,
severed phone cords disconnect
the conversation we could never start.

Eggplants grow woody stems
and resist the flexible truth that bends
from bridges to rivers and back.
Forever, over even the moment's sun
and lasting clouds between now and when,
eggplants grow woody stems
and resist the flexible truth that bends.

THAT OTHER NIGHT WHEN

dark crunches down
behind some planet
waiting to jump puddles
time seize land masses
swallow rivers flatten
mountains freeze lava
until we surrender willingly
to its subversive seduction
embrace folds contours
planes of existence
dimensions of imagination
suppressed memories
then skipping over
an impossible sea
to an unknown continent
over remote tributaries
beyond shadow peaks
we burn with cold

COMES THE DARKNESS

Quietly, as early dusk drops dark's dust,
Winter waits around the corner, wispy
wedding gown blowing, an over-dressed
mugger ready to crack the year's shortest day
across our hibernation-drugged heads.

Another prognosis that so much we want
to be wrong: another cousin, friend, lover
covered in ice, frozen solid before
Spring sculpts—something borrowed, something
taken—with each breath, each arctic-air gust.

Sometimes, it is almost too much to carry.
Winter wants to let the guilt go, to escape
to the Caribbean, lay on the beach, get a tan.
Sometimes, the job seems holy: cleaning
slate for the next seasons' lecturers.

After the solstice starts, though, the nights
slowly grow smaller, reflecting in their recession
on the long march into our consciousness.
Orange windows punctuate the velvet silences
like the tiny sounds of a symphony's triangle.

They sing: go ahead, fall in love or lust.
Let the world slowly be created again.
Sing or swirl across the open fields
like snowflakes in a blizzard's hands.
Just don't expect this life to last.

APOCALYPTIC WINTER

Murk clenches around the world—
solstice, yes, cruor, surely, necrosis,
certainly—trees pull back to their roots,

plants close for business,
even cockroaches go dormant
or almost sleep through the night.

Those few flowers on a windowsill
only admonish me in the name of the
painted flood that stained last summer.

Dried herbs crumble, anamnesis of the sun.
I stop, though, and talk to the feral cat
whose felicitations hiss out from iron bars

on top of a stone wall that divides civic
sidewalk from exclusive parking. I would
purr, unlike this ginger gamine cat,

if I had cause enough to speak.
The thalassic truth of this spot sidesteps
my yearning to swim in the desert.

Absinthian coffee wakes something
harsh and green, but not for long, and my
bleak bones creep forth on a nameless road.

The moon climbs, you want me to offer
straightaway. *A ray penetrates the dark day
and lifts the crux to spheres surmounting*

*dictionaries and thesauri that spill
obfuscations, tangle moods and modes
into articulate modifications of noumena.*

The cat didn't lie, so neither will the eye.
Clouds hid the moon. An uncanny aura
spilled down. The trees gamboled slowly,

lifting their roots and dropping them, a
geographic gamble. Stories stumbled down
cliffs. Nothing changed in the seething

and nothing persisted unchanged, which
I don't apprehend. The tongue does
not construe such spectacles or words.

I REMEMBERED DREAMING

Once we dreamt, I don't know *what,*
just conjure *that.* Like sun-warmed
rain in a dilatory rill, it refreshed our
feet. A blue feather wafts down as we
perch there—a bit of sky, flight, truth.
Vacant nights besiege us, nothing
more than a dried orange peel found
in a kitchen corner or white garlic skin
discovered sliding in the air along
the floor. The pips did not grow;
the bulb might have sprung up
green shoots, but these shriveled
as we slept. Who breathes like this,
loud and rasping, as though reaching
for a finish line that recedes from
my grasp? Hungers outnumber
dreams now. Peckish imagination
arises out of habit and unfulfilled
desire. Unrepentant love once
lived under a roof of dreams,
but it took a broom and a mop
to clean up after the squall. So
we thatched our lives together
and slept under rising planets
and a cyclic moon. We hiked
where we could and found springs
from time to time. An acacia
provided scant shade when we
chose to sit. Sketches recollect
contrast and contradiction, rush-
hour delays on the way to work,
reality emerging from the sand.
Now, we decant wine from broken
promises and pronounce decrees
in the desert with dusty cant. Yes,
once we dreamt. That, I remember.
I mean, then, I remembered. Now, I can't.

THIS ANCIENT PLACE WHERE MY FOOTSTEPS LEAVE NO TRACE

This ancient place where
my footsteps leave no trace,
dust covering dust as
hot winds blow from
far deserts to mere
shadows cast by the
wet Western planes of
the Mediterranean basin.

I have never lived so far
from water. Did I already
tell you this? Or felt
so rootless. I've taken
photos of those roots
that break through rocks,
cracking apart the hills
they grasp so hungrily.

It could be greed.
Did you ever think
about that? My grip
weakens, as though
slipping from the hot
rock, unable to keep
from falling off
a cliff into

the Salt Sea, unable
to sink in this sea that is
unable to sustain life.
Unable to break
through the hard
surface of things
and let sweet water
in, I breathe

sulfurous fumes
as this earth rejects
an outsider.
Stunted trees
shrivel in heat
above broken
stone. Somehow,
I amble on. Do I say
this a lot? Do you
think about this?

UP AGAINST THE WALL,

…sits an odd statuary, a sullen sadness
created by hand from nothing more or less
than general failures that anyone might
turn away from on some given day:

A house taken by bankers who would not
settle for anything less from two buyers,
work taken by a promise never meant,
a culture and language unfathomably

resistant to my resistance, failed art
unsold, books stacked in dusty piles
waiting for non-existent readers.
Walk away. We all walk away, they say.

Leave it alone. It doesn't mean anything—
home, career, art—those broken fragments
of a mirror that once reflected a token self.
Now they sculpt a dark fear, emptiness,

this heavy statue, unwilling or unable
to step, sing, or share in the world
of carefree surrender—a listening post
that monitors the cries of a million children,

refugees, the screams of thousands
a day sacrificed in violence to bastard wars
that go on unacknowledged—a conflagration
of our nightmares—the continuing

struggles against razor wire, bullets,
land mines, rape, hunger, thirst—
all of the many other varied bacterial
and viral symptoms of the human syndrome.

Silence stands statue-still, hidden,
up against the depression in a stone wall
built two-thousand years ago, like
a crumpled piece of paper tucked

safely in a crack, only a plea full of desire
and passion for the healing of a world
that rejects all offers, takes your work,
confuses languages, destroys art, burns books.

Five-hundred years ago the paper slipped
from my fingers, out of reach, into this wall
that holds up contention and strife of a contested
land loved in the name of fallen grace, believing

a small moment may yet revive a spark:
a sprig of lavender picked along the way,
a simple tune hummed in passing,
your quiet summer smile freely given.

TIME SLIPS INTO A DREAM AND RETURNS THE FAVOR

My dear friend and teacher, you slipped quietly into my dream last night,
with an up-to-date haircut fitting that yet unnamed generation
that comes after the one now rising. I complimented you, noting
to myself how you were now younger than I, the dream erasing
nearly a score of years between us. *That's good to hear,*
your once familiar voice boomed, *for civil wars rage at home.*

> /for civil wars wage at home
> there is no poetry in this—yet—
> tired, deeply tiered towers
> lean out and in/

This sounds familiar, I allow, and though you seemed surprised, I let you in on
something of my own domesticated conflict. War stories that no one believed,
in the usual terms of economics, freedom, morality. We were great orators,
then.

> /mostly missing people, connection
> who am i
> empty/

You smiled, just before I woke with only fragments of your last remark—
…this morning…in the garden…—and now more comes to me:

You saw a wheelbarrow you left out through winter,
sun had come around it to touch some ice in its shadow all this while.

When I saw the ice melting, you said. I think, "Ah, now some hope
returns to the world." I couldn't wake fully from this dream.

> /wheel barrow
> Williams' *so much depends upon*
> > so much depends upon going to bed,
> > sleeping, coming to this later
> > dream and not to dream

per
chance
a lottery ticket/

I try to piece the dream together with my waking world. Your name, my friend,
had come up in conversation, we will see each other soon, and, yes,

there had been conflict in my first marriage, now over.

Suzannah has been writing from England where she worries about her son's
education.
She thinks war is coming in America, which surprises me. Is it safe to bring
Zach here?

She wants to know, for she's heard about guns and drugs in schools.

There is the fall yard-work to be done, a need for wheelbarrows—
and my tendency to leave things not done…not put away…

　　　/images—dark, light

　　senses—
　　　　　　smell—garden, fall, spring melt
　　　　　　see—light on wheelbarrow, dark violent streets
　　　　　　touch—cold, hot, a man's back
　　　　　　hear—shots, oration, cries, the rhythm of the automatic
　　　　　　　　　weapons
　　　　　　taste—

　　sensation/

oh, what do you taste,
the bitter fruit of labor
or the lack,
oh bitter dark roots
rotted at the ends,
the timbers fall, you fall,

this death, this death
this end of teaching
lessons un-learned
falling apart around
the pieces, a dream

>   /Cohen sings *the stories of the street are mine*
>   and Dylan cries *the times they are a'changin'*
>   echoing around Stevens' *not the last war, the next/*

This, then, I return
to you, dear teacher—
choose the best answer
for this exam

>   A. tractor fumes
>   B. humid wind
>   C. rustling corn
>   D. settling furrows
>   E. leaves' whirring wings
>   F. hunting gunshots' blast

>   smell of gunpowder cliché

cordite cords tie
a band around
our reasoning
hearts

the dog sighs, waiting
for me to return
to the place where I belong

>   /unformed
>   formed
>   unknown
>   known

i can't write
i cant write
i can write
icon write
cant write
Kant write
i must write/

there is nothing
but glib air
floating inside
my lungs,

the cavities of my body filled
ghosts of useless pop songs
no one wants to hear

/desperation-train heading
for the collapsing bridge
or the dark Freudian tunnel

desire oh desire
whom do you desire
who desires you?
who desires me?
who, oh who desires me?
not my body. oh, that, too/

but me, who am nothing
does nothing
thinks no thought that is not an echo
of some other song

/despair
anxiety
angst
eyed a tee/

i just want to spend
some time alone with
oh

you

        /no one would
        quiet, alone/

Well, my teacher, this is not what you expected, is it?
Whose dream un-dreams here
and creates nothing
but word-salad tossed
under through the computer buss,
a barrow of monkey funds
yet no one stands anymore

        /someone who sees me
        as I see me
        would not want
        to be me/

motionless, I have no reflection
in the mirror I am an emotional vampire

Dear teacher, teach me one last lesson,
one last lesson that cannot be undone.

I must write but no more tonight

        /perhaps the sun rises to
        turn me into a hissing vat
        of tempestuous steam

        vacuous steam on an autumn night
           like fog on Jerusalem's streets
           a moon three-quarters full

full-throated, looking as though
it would drop from the sky/

at any moment
through the fog
that might or might not
to me be many, much
me/s/s/ too

and so I slip back
into night under blanket
and all of this ten years ago
now, and then, a decade to come.
And now, now the decades drop one
by one from the crack between night and day.
And civil war may yet come.

TEACHERS

For my children

i
Teachers come to us again and again
and we learn from them what we will.
We give them in return only a
thin immortality. We hope for gentleness.

We dream of our old teachers often.
The bullies shout, "get the lead out"
as every muscle concentrates
on the knowledge that we cannot win this race.

ii
Teachers come to us again and again
and we learn from them what we will.
We give them in return only a
thin immortality. We hope for gentleness.

The gentle ones quietly step away,
letting go as we pedal furiously and discover
that miraculously we have found balance
while pushing forward to the next road.

iii
We sat at table eating *phô*, another lunch
where you ask questions that I never thought.
I try to catch these waves as they break toward shore
and wonder that you came to me last night in a dream.

In our own teaching, we find our voices
raised all too often. Yet, somehow, I step
back as you light into a world I will
not know, unless you take me along.

UNEQUAL NIGHT

i

Yesterday came the equinox
while a solar eclipse made
night somewhat longer,
and later, suicide bombers
killed (at least) one-hundred
thirty-seven in Sanaa, making
the night mightier than the equal
day. Today UNESCO celebrates
world poetry day.

ii

        We should
declare poetry night. Without
some darkness, poems
could fade away. Without
a little poetry, the darkness
would overcome what day-
light we have left, return
us to the long, cold, nuclear
winter of our nightmares.

CALLED TO FAITH

A man stands over the culvert on the gravel road onto the farm.
The stone he hefts in his hand—igneous remnants from before time,
bits of crystal cooled across history mingled with impurities beyond memory.
He lofts this shard of the past in a slow arc that ends in the dark standing water.

Sometimes he wishes he could follow,
down through the water as surface tension
erases faint traces; he wishes sometimes that
he could fall through the cold numbness
to sink into the soft, welcoming mud—
to sleep among layers of last year's rotting leaves
and the year's before and the year's before and years' before—
layers of organic memory that,

still,

do not reach the stone's most recent memory.
The stone takes no notice. And the man
does not sink with the stone into murkiness.
The morning calls him to his desire,
so he chooses to return to the work at hand.
There is a garden to plow and disk.
There is corn to plant and tend.
There are nettles to uproot and remove.

Despite the threat of frost or hail or rabbit or deer, he trusts
that in August there will be sweet corn and tomatoes and beans.
He will gather some in and eat. He will gather some in to store. And
he will gather the best for next year's seeds. These make up his act of love.

LAND/ 'SCAPE/ MEMORY

More than a decade ago he sold the farm,
not that he really farmed except
to plant a few thousand trees.
He won't see that crop come in.

The farmhouse casts a shadow in his dreams.

Now the house will go, the one in the city.
The banks will have it one way or another,
either through courts or through a sale
that does not cover the hole of his debt.

There is not much to think about this.

These houses will not leave his nights:
the city-house's oak buffet, hardwood floors,
clematis in the garden in all shapes
and shades; the expanse around the country house.

A lack of space shrink-wraps his chest, squeezes lungs.

He used to hike for the air and the wide
horizons, in the Negev and on Mount Hermon,
by the Red Sea and in the Western Plains. His knees
collapsed under the weight, though.

Now he walks sometimes into the fields

he used to own, in his dreams, when the new
owner is not home. It is winter and the moisture
of his expiration freezes into sparks of light
that float through the air like imagination.

He looks out over the cold beaver pond.

The frozen surface lifts over the field,
dripping water and cold fish into the crater
below. And the trees listen, listen, listen.
In the morning there will be work
to be done.
          But he will wait for tomorrow.

Silent rivers do not refill their flow

into the ocean, drying up one by one.
The oceans overflow beaches, flood
flatlands, turn against mountains—
islands escape to memory's landscape.

He walks quietly on, bidding farewell.

The ice drops back. It will crack
into a million pieces. Who knows?
Who knows? Trees remain listening,
glistening in a glissando of icy remains.

Napping in a chair

MEMORIES

Ice crusts Autumn snow
but underneath, mud.
A phone grows cold,
finger of memory
reaching for
obsolete dial.
Touch something now,
not forgotten.
Leather-coat smell
wraps around
a few moments.
These few drops
grow, crystallize.
Snowflakes fall
at night.

SONG

I walked through flame, steamed up,
rose into the ionosphere and froze to rare ice,
swirled in winter blizzards around your knees
and melted into the living ground that struggled
      to breathe beneath your feet.

I suffocated under poured concrete, turned rancid and rotted to dust,
drank gasoline and sought sparks again and again
until I exploded, bloody fissure inside your chest—

a silenced gun-shot in an empty room.
And the snore of sleeping you never woke from—
was the tv on?
     Did you watch?

MYSTERY MAN

Someone's always offering a better way,
selling or buying or giving it away at the fruit stand:
Won't you stay with me today?

Colors in the rain, down the window pane play
on their way to some greener plan.
Someone's always offering a better way.

A budding tree draws you with its sway,
but you do not bruise the flower with your hand:
Won't you stay with me today?

Come with me, lay down this day.
I'm another mystery man,
someone always offering a better way

to live, to love, to die, to pray. Despite
branches of you that I do not understand—
will you stay with me today?

Always some traveling man purveys:
Won't you join my caravan?
Someone always offers a better way,
but will you stay by me, today?

FUZZY LOGIC

Fuzz inside my head,
like mold, clouds
thinking & I nod
off without dreams
in the desert sun,
drying out.

EMILY

To pull a Curtain back—
Peeking out on that black Street—
Where Flames have scorched the Hills and screamed
At seventy miles-per-hour down the Turnpike—
Trotted out by mushroom Shapes—

And splintered your Nice Duplex at Number five-five-six.
It's too late to cry—
To put that Current back even
As your Brain slips its Groove—
This Nightmare Variation

One you never dreamed of.
Don't let that Curtain go—
Keep this Vision tight in your Hand
And draw the Horror down through you—
In this quiet, dark Land.

BAROMETRIC PRESSURE DROPPING

Clouds pace across the sun, ice shadows
chilling ground where they block the light—
shadows—

like blood stains on a prayer shawl,
pooled blood on the floor—
dark stains—

waiting for people to drink it up,
taste fear, feed the deep anger—
ancient

rage burning like the sun
behind the coming storm—
ruins—

what brought breath now consumes it.

SILENT POETRY, APRIL 21, 1988

The dark blue wind of early autumn
ran on the early autumn sky… —Robert Frost, "Sleep Impression"

i   Dust blasted in the wind dries my mouth and words fall
away, autumn's leaves scraping pavement on their way
to being caught in grass filament.

I don't know what to say to you about distances,
money, crackling leaves and filtered dust, white sand
that has not been said before, fast and easy.

I do not know what to say to you about silence—
because I don't know it, but it pushes me
like the wind into the soft green tendrils of your arms.

I drift on the lake bottom, with the white sand,
and on the surface with the dry leaves, soaking up
water but not able to fathom the distance between us.

ii   Silence outside of your door, inside your room,
falls across the floor, a dark shadow.
I reach to touch your olive skin, you
asleep in the dark night, illumined
by the strobe flash of the mute TV.

Your breath whispers in the silence—a regular, quiet
plea—never singing out to fill the shadows
with the light of your holy passion.

I cannot feel you anymore, the space
has become so huge, and your once throbbing
body breathes so deeply, it fades into shadow.
I turn the TV off, walk downstairs.
Night birds call and I answer.

iii   Dusk, and clouds obscure evening heat
lightning across the river and miles away—
I wish it was the bright moon, that odd dream-
shade opposite to the midnight-sun and blue-dawn color
that surrounded it outside my window early this morning.
The orange circle stunned me so that I woke you up and asked
you to witness the world—the orange circle a sun deep beneath a
perfect sea, heat lightning cooled and purified and poured into coin.
I wish my silence was that cool moon, encompassed by its complement
blue. I wish it would wake you up, *dark blue wind*. I wish it would wake
you up and you would say, "How beautiful!"

SHACKLETON ON THE WEST COAST
OF SOUTH GEORGIA ISLAND

To arrive at this beach, impossible. Not yet saved, though.
Behind, vengeful waves scream for blood;
ahead, glaciers tremble at the thought of warm flesh,
ready to clamp terrible fissures around a meager meal.

Which way? Crushing through waves in shattered,
jury-rigged lifeboat? Or crashing across cragged silence?
And what of the skin-shredding, unforgiving wind?
Both courses certain cataclysm, one path must lead to deliverance.

Shackleton wrenched screws through the soles of his boots,
ascended treacherous ice and stone, slid down
to civilization—a small fishing camp nestled in a barren bight.
He distrusted the sea's thirst all too much.

But perhaps this is Shackleton's secret:
Both paths lead to redemption, sooner or later—
freezing waves or roaring glaciers, destruction or rescue,
all the same in the end. It doesn't matter which direction.

Only that we choose.

THESE PAST NIGHTS

(after Robert Duncan)

ring round the cemetery moon
or future prediction
of weather or distance

                 or joining together

a predilection for diffusion
diffraction the breaking up   of reflected meaning
in an ice crystal dance   configuration
in confusion   the rarefied air dream life—death

to touch   dark warmth   melt

dissolving moon dogs into night
teaming with stars   —stark moonlight
measured   in angstroms
arbiters of   meaninglessness

ON READING ROBERT DUNCAN

                                                 trying to

      unravel Duncan's Attis   ◊   who could be Osiris,

      a christ immortal wound   ◊   or Adonis,

             head in stars

                clay shrouded feet,

                    revived, dancing the beat

                       ◊

slipping back to old book lists, I read

                Memphis

             of the Eagle

of the Lion   ◊   of the Bull,

            part human

        ◊ each part of ◊

     yellow sun-flare pentacle flashing

              auric.

               ◊

        A healing mixture

   ◊ clove, ambergris, frankincense, myrrh ◊

             musk

        of bodies merged

       in humid embrace

             ◊

        and dreaming

   ◊ Jeffers' eagle soars with grace resurrected ◊

   ◊ blooded peacock hanging from its hoary claws ◊

Bruised bodies bathed in aloe massage   ◊

on the hot beach, turquoise shore   ◊

swim through her more and less   ◊

immersed and lost in the warm wet   ◊

salt and sea creatures
mermaid　　　◊　　　merman
mysteries
◊
lost without legs to dance
◊

FRACTURES

i
The whole dark vessel shattered, at first.
So full of possible light, it exploded
into stars, galaxies, planets, solar
systems, down to grains of sand
and dust. Wipe the dust off your
smooth surfaces, your imperfect
vases. Make them shine like fire
from the Big Bang. Someone
shaped that container from clay,
organic mud left over from a life
you never knew. It doesn't matter.

ii
Massive collisions excite all
of the sub-atomic particles
into jumping from atomic shell
to sea shell, hermit crabs
searching for a larger, more
powerful residence. And we
live life like this, don't we?
Looking for the home
we believe will shelter us
while we outgrow it, while we
still defend its borders, walls.

iii
See my skin, my language?

iv
Speaking of language,
have you thought of
a song to sing? We
call the fragments
differences, these
simple vessel-bits,
eight puzzle dimensions

that make a song.
If you grind them down,
they still orbit something.
Quantum revolution excites me.

v
You and I could burn
like suns, change shells.

vi
If we continue to
destroy justice then we
will only be left with more
pieces to fit back together.
I should not scuttle across
ocean floors looking for
the homes of the dead.
Electrons rise above
surfaces, fly into emptiness.
But quantum spaces of this page create
the possibilities of our friendship.

vii
We reach a resting state.

viii
The emptiness of the universe will wait.

SOMEWHERE, A WHIRRING FAN

"With this beginning, the unknown concealed one created the palace. This palace is called אלוהים *(Elohim), God.* The secret is: בראשית ברא אלוהים *(Bereshit bara Elohim), With beginning, _____ created God* (Genesis 1:1)."

— *Zohar* (I:15a)

"…She knows that her beloved is searching for her; so what does she do? She opens the portal to her hidden room [in the palace] slightly and reveals her face for a moment, and then hides it again."

— *Zohar* (II.99a)

Somewhere, a whirring fan
in an open window spins
possibilities into threads.
I heard a rumor that the
Oleander flowers shed
their pink and white grace
for poisonous reason.
A car slinks down traces
of a melted tar road.

You like to stand by the window,
and want him to see you there,
behind a curtain. He doesn't
know you or you him. He walks
the span of street, infrequently
catching a glimpse of blue
eyes, a reflection in cracks
of the cotton-hued skies.

The crow calls from a tree.
Another day, green parrots
screech louder than the
traffic flees. The heat lays
like a corpse upon our city.
Bougainvillea bracts spot
gardens with false hope,
colorful arrays of forgotten
pain turned to sweet honey.

He forgets you, though you
never meet. And you, also,
forget—window, curtains,
the desire for a stranger's
glad glance. Someone wants
this to be autobiography, a
short recollection of moments
actually lived. That person never
dreamed, does not exist anymore.

And I never existed because I
don't stop dreaming. Poetry, like
a god, provides code for an image,
keying it to suggest a revelation-lode
from your past. You want it to be
my past. Parrots screech.
A crow calls. A beautiful Other
by the window waits. This all
happens to you while I write

these scenes tangled in dreams,
whirring fans—the poem unable
to light any form, your reading,
this page; unable to discover more
than bare wisps of meaning in the
vibrations of words—your song longing
for someone in the infinite void. Wanting
a mortal to read you into this, to see you
alive, you seek a new beginning—genesis.

Note: *Zohar* refers to *The Book of Splendor,* one of the main texts of the Kabbalah.

THURSDAY

The bruised shadows of evening
sea gulls stretch out along the ground.
Bells ring them in, holding them near
to the town tucked against mountains
of a notorious shore.

                      When we were
best friends still, we would walk
along the water, watching the sun
set at the intersection of peninsula
and sea.

        As lovers we lived in the dark,
that deep purple shade of shadows
on the wall of my room.

                      So, the cry
of gulls rains down at dusk.
Earlier, I said goodbye
                  to you.

Now, I will go to the edge of the land
and watch the evening come.

NAPPING IN A CHAIR

Yesterday seagulls laughed
under the storm clouds caught
in mountains behind the sea.

As I ambled through a plaza,
I heard someone playing piano
stop and start the music over.

People ate lunch, drank coffee.
The rain did not fall on them or
anyone. The ships slid slowly by.

I noticed these things. I did not
notice other things. I thought of
you, I am not sure why. I walked.

I heard sea gulls, a piano, the sea.
I listened for echoes of your voice.
I remembered something you said.

As I neared the wharf, fish swam near me.
Only faint shadows revealed them.
Two lovers sat under trees conversing.

I thought of someone. I don't recall who.

SING THIS AT THE END

for Michael Dennis Browne

Like a flight of flamingos
scattering over fish ponds,
my life careened.
Like a moment
in the dunes, wild tulips
glowing red,
my life sailed.
Like sand hitting my face,
lifted by winter gales,
my life left scars.
Rain arrowed down
amid lightning, thunder;
the wind invigorated my life.
Like a dark night in August
when sirens wail,
torpor filled my life.
In a word, a minute's heat,
I discovered passion.
You know the sun, as it falls
from beneath gloomy clouds
into the sea?
My life stretched
its fingers like that.
It is not so much
to consider these.
Like a Sabbath rest,
my life unfolds each day.

Flying without dice

GEESE

*"We have become familiar with geese," an old woman's voice laughed.
"I have slipped on goose poop, let me tell you."*
—Heard on Minnesota Public Radio, 14 February, 1992.

They return each year to watch—
arrowheads dart across the bottoms of clouds,
overhead the cacophony of petty disagreement, as geese
call to each other, repeating past
errors and folly.

They return each year to overhear—
laughter, melancholy blend— ghost-dragons
gryphoned with waddling pigs— calls, dented saxophones—
chased by over-eager children— they signal
a singular faith.

Geese return South each year—
swimming in warm water they only
dreamed of when they started out, still young,
arguing best routes and who would fly
point next trip.

Each year, when they return—
an old couple migrates to the lake shore; they discuss
with geese the relatedness of things, the affirmation of gripes
and grumps. Skin thickened, ears deaf,
they keep warm.

This year they return—
the man's wrinkles feather out, his trunk still tall;
the woman slips on shit, her laughing voice a bow-string release.
Now she will say— *We have become familiar
with geese.*

Next year they may not return—
Winter does not defeat them, though.
The old come offering corn, bread and company:
the geese become fat cupids, feeding—
droppings everywhere.

They will not return next year—
skin molting, eyes dim, they whisper to the geese—
                              We think we understand.
Geese release them to fly away,
fly away home—

NIGHT WAVES

Moonlight
as a windstorm
Uproots trees
waves buildings
Twists roads
unsteadies feet
Stirs brown trees through
their own green leaves
Then strains to follow

STORM

A figure shrugs on a shroud,
hair challenging streaks of creosote.
Its path follows steep cliffs—

in black smoky wreaths swirling—
whose further depths disturb the
seductive sea below smashing

towards the sky, wrapping around
the bruised, solemn night, trapping many.
White foam and mist rise from its mouth—

red flames from its eyes
hide dry leaves, lies, life—
cold steam against dark heat.

SKETCH

Lines never quite
converge. Perspective.
Memory, representations
of her mouth, her nose,
consuming her face.
Her hair would cover
invisible ears. Why
can't I draw a mouth—
fears? I long to lick
the question-mark
ridge, to kiss her
speaking lips.

DRAWING BREATH(LESS)

A bit stretched,
this line we pen between life
and death, between life
and life. Sometimes
our own. Sometimes
another's.

Elongated,
my legs akimbo on the couch,
reading some poetry, a novel,
a bit of or a bitter philosophy.
You sip coffee in the morning—
maybe wine, if evening
falls while we.

Opening up
the locked cabinet we find as usual
an emptiness familiar, comforting—
vacuumed of emotions, better.
Like work and social
gatherings, where
we pretend.

We pretend.
Something involving chocolate,
painted skin, holding
each other apart,
against centripetal forces,
tight petals of a flower
pressed into bursting buds.

Reaching stars
when standing, that is, seeing
them, tired, failing to drink enough.
Glimpses of intimacy obscured
and hidden while seeming to
reveal. Grief in a game of
hide and seek.

I don't know if
you or I will ever understand. This.
Perhaps I am in the psychiatric ward
again. Where I used to work. Or perhaps
you are in rehab, for your failure to drink
enough alcohol to fuel the economy.
Forgetfulness sells.

In recollections
such as these nothing can be found,
everything lost forgets where it lived,
death lives and life, well, you know.
Toss rounded river stones into
a pile, skip some flat stones
over resting water.

In recollections,
I don't know if,
reaching stars,
we pretend—
opening up,
elongated,
a bit stretched.

THE END OF THE DAY

In a light rain of cold needles, I tracked
the long walk downstairs, out the door,
along the curved road toward the gate—
trudging, really, as though knowing there,
where knowing was no escape. Gray

slid into darker and darker suits, drenched
now, slippery and shiny as the lights sparked
into orange, their existential moods—warm, lonely,
cold, yet friendly, all at once. This life sentence,
punctuated by red tail lights and white headlight

dashes along, drops under the snaking tires its stretched
burden of long, thin months between visiting hours.
We seek solace and comfort, but settle for a few
short nods of rest in the warm cab on the way home—
the familiar long journey toward the end of the day.

NEIGBHOR'S SHIVA

Monday, when I venture out,
the sign next door
announces my neighbor's death.

I never met him. I'm only
saying this, you know.
I mean, I'm subletting
and he never went out
and I haven't even
been here a month.

When I return,
          I hear the mourners'
prayers through thin walls, and
wonder what they might hear.

In the evening, I go
          to a wedding.

FOR IRWIN GOOEN

...for man goes to his everlasting home,
and the mourners go about in the street.
—Kohelet 12:5

The door closed. Clouds cover the moon;
the rain a memory blocking out the stars.
Desire has drained into the trembling house,
tools disused gather dust. Seeing nothing
out the windows, the house wraps dark arms
around the one in his old chair, quiet now.
Some music might have played, but his lovers
forgot the words and did not sing anymore.
Higher on the ridge, a lone bird calls alarm.

The mills on the river below fall in on themselves.
But apple trees still blossom, lilacs scent the air.
The oxygen tube shines silver, snapped
like a cord, unneeded. A pitcher of water
fell, crashing into the silence. At dawn,
a golden light suffuses the house, the man's
body empty in his favorite chair. His fountain of
words evaporates off the wall where he wrote them.
The wheels have fallen from the truck.

When his friends find him, they lay him
beneath the stone he carved.

And the dust returns to the earth
as it was, and the spirit returns to God,
Who gave it.
—Kohelet 12:7

Note: *Kohelet* is the Hebrew name for *The Book of Ecclesiastes.*

YESTERDAY

for Pansy Bradshaw

Parents of an infant girl
prayed in thanks at the *Kotel*
after so many years believing
they "didn't merit" a child—
the weather nice, reasonably
warm for October.

                    At the light
rail stop an angry man turned
the wheel and sped his car
into people waiting.

The three-month old girl
sprang into the air when
the car her stroller struck.
But she did not land—
only her clothes fell down
like white, dropped petals
on the table cloth.

An old man-nanny
fell for her, in Montana
I think it was. His body
collapsed to earth. His
spirit grabbed hers. He
carried her into the sky
as his brain bled for her.

He turned blue, grew
wings and flew—a
violin under his chin.
A goat standing on
the roof of a yellow
shed saw.

A small red bird
rested on his shoulder,
the air filled with color—
speckled bubbles,
sefirot of an artist's
imagination contracting
and expanding to burst.

The weather was nice
for October and his love
for children too great to let
her fall. It was the only
thing that he could do,
one last painting that
he wanted to give you.

Notes: The *Kotel* is the Hebrew name for The Western Wall of the Temple Mount, in
Jerusalem.
Sefirot are emanations, mystical-sacred light (*Or*), which flow through
attributes by which *The Infinite (En Sof)* reveals itself.

AT THE CEMETERY

for Hannah and for Haviv, z"l

The distraught woman bends over
the disturbed ground, screaming
at the man just interred there—
cries of good-bye and how-could-you,

pulled from deep inside, sent down
deeper to reach through hard scrabble,
rock, sand—reaching for the deaf ears
to call them back with sound and tears.

Around her, other women punctuate
their consternation with cries and sobs,
while his widow's hand, alone and silent,
quietly drops a stone along the grave's edge—

marking the uncrossable perimeter
separating her from the man she married
at sixteen. Their children call out while
the grandchildren stand stunned.

And the sun, rudely golden and beautiful,
touches trees on the western side
of the valley. Jerusalem continues,
not noticing when a thin silence falls.

YOU MAY NOT WANT TO READ THIS, BUT

i
whoever said, *nothing is carved in stone,*
never visited the graveyard full of flowering

rock newly carved, and old granite—petals
faded and leaning—ready to fall to the ground.

ii
After thirty days we check that the clouds
of mourning read out loud have not stained

the setting stone, that the dead remain dead,
held down by geological history and time, rocks

iii
torn from the ground weighing them, keeping
them from rising up again to claim the messiah

and all the ancestors and descendants.
They scream their names out loud for those

iv
who forgot and whisper soft condolences to
those who remember when blood pumped,

breath laughed, and eyes sparked—
shades of joy for each of us, in our turn.

AFTER VISITING THE CEMETERY IN THE SNOW…

I've restarted many a wood stove's flames
from sleeping embers when the firebox
remained warm. In the darkening evening,
a faint glow glimmers beneath snowy ash.
We watch it as sleep seeps into our veins.
Some stone tablets I suppose say the
Phoenix rises from ashes. But I cannot
catch those who sleep below the tinder's
reach, or rekindle those beyond the oak's
broken trunk, which spirits signals into the sky—
all red streamers, white steam, black smoke.

AUTUMN MILKWEED

When I die, bury my body
amid a pile of leaves,
then go home.
Plant clematis vines along fences,
fill the rest of your yard
with only native flowers
that will desire compost—
tend them lovingly,
as though you had cared for me.

NOTHING REMEMBERS

where in our times we these rocks piled into buildings
that fell down a thousand years ago dis(re)membered from war
or earthquake raised and razed again into where nothing
recalls again the warm day anemones bloom hollyhocks
poppies forget no one and another rain day another dry day
pass hot and cold while an *orvani* drops blue feathers in flight
a hawk sits calmly on a fencepost and flocks of egrets
traipse toward the sea no cattle no grains all harvested
in this place we would call holy land nothing left to it but conflict
with the passing of her life that tried so hard to hang onto one
moment many moments missed so many more empty echoes
a difficult way to say goodbye to a mother watching her
evaporate like rain in the desert her mind dust that dries
lips her droned words faded as warmth from a midnight rock
meaning what the layers of history these rocks un-piled
reveal sepia photos a couple of tin-types dust school
reports cards newspaper holes the shells of bugs raised and razed
again and again into our times where nothing remembers

DUST TO DUST

Sleep and dream fly
off together—dish and spoon
beneath the cowed moon—
and wonder if daisies die
when the wine turns to dust.

Surfaces fluster dust,
flitter across our screens—
revealing the hidden lust
of light-and-shadow scenes—
old celluloid ideas crumbling.

Eyelids crumble like old film, flicker—
resist pulsating wakefulness.
Waves stream behind a boat—quicker
currents spraying—nonetheless
entropy glosses the lake's surface.

Flies surface on a glossy window—
crowded dun specks—each self-hurled,
hard, up against the dull winter glow—
drummers selling speculation that our world
will flicker to dust, surface in sleep and dreams.

FLYING WITHOUT DICE

Not the odds, probability or possibility,
walking along a stream, waterfalls ahead;
nor sitting in mountain wind as the airport
slips away under the noise of clocks
forgetting the ticks that flock memory;
not geese in Oneonta's skies—beneath duck's
distressed, convening cackles; nor a wood
stove dancing passion as gasses
stream carbonaceous oblivion along
meridians calculated to deceive
a sense of order, a few imaginary
boundaries of time. So simpler to
receive the deception of hours while
sensing movement toward a finality
that constantly slips into tomorrow
until tonight comes—in the deep
slumbering giant silhouette-shaped
mountain range: a pass, a saddle,
a horse racing toward immortality,
limitless dreams fleeing past oaks
blown down in the wind shear,
storm of oblivion, dust, smoke.

Flying bound—aluminum, magnesium,
sodium chlorides, ferrous sulphates,
collide tidally among waves below—
the sea we cross from continent to
embattled continental plate, cracked
and distorted, a rift in sensibility—
sensuous signal of hot sulphur—springs
to life, dehydrates into burning
logos, which desires mountains.
Trees, cracked and crackling, cry
out with screams, delight sparks
through the flue, invisible against
night skies. Jet aircraft roars over
soft piano jazz tango of the tangled

words: expressionless, blank, white
fonts floating in milk, reflected clouds
giving the illusion of a full moon,
the circle at the well's top, the dark
clear water blued into green, self-portrait
shadow leaning over the stone-lined hole.

Reading Mexican poetry translated,
hearing untranslated Hebrew voices,
piano chords surrealistic eros, evolution
swims from the portals of splashing
planes in the curved sea ragged with waves:

Not the possibility or probability,
not the odds walking past
(the lottery ticket window)—
just bumpy air and rough decks
predicting nothing as the Tarot
reader considers by chance
a favor she once held in the palm
of her hand. The sun rose from
the middle of the body's night,
drawing a margin of dawn
slated for sleep. A dripping distant
pendulum swings over a trussed
buxom heroine who laughs that yet
again the siren-wail saxophone-
imagined piano pauses, punctuating
sentences judged too heavy or light
among falling currencies, unslung
from tired shoulders. Still, we trudge
along hoping for the rising night
to rescue our exhausted ardor—
breathless, fatigued, silent.

Silence and poetry at the center
of rushing-engine screams

lays hands on us and prays
for listeners, discovering the
lack of oxygen in the air of
history, the thin cold atmosphere
compressed beneath wings.
Theory holds us up,
a thin blanket over our legs,
a neck pillow resisting stiffly
any hint of rest. Like old geese,
I migrate in memory, metallically
tapping a tin-drum heart in a blank
man's chest, smaller than the eye
of the sparrow flitting beneath
our table at the cafe that last
day at the beach when the
pigeons stole the French fries
and threw away the foam box.

The wind came up.
The sand blew away.

Yet, against
all odds, we speak,
and, sometimes,
we understand—
or almost.
Even more odd,
sometimes
we don't need to.

Acknowledgments

Many poems in this collection were first published (sometimes in an earlier version) in the following places:

After visiting the cemetery in the snow. *The Bookends Review.*
Apocalyptic Winter, Called to Faith, Drawing Breath(less), For Irwin Gooen, I
   Remembered Dreaming, Sitting Shiva. *The BeZine.*
At the Cemetery. *Margutte: Non-rivista online di letteratura e altro.*
Autumn Milkweed. *Abramelin: the Journal of Poetry and Magick. The BeZine.*
Blue notes. *The Best of Northlight 1990.*
Comes the Darkness, Flying Without Dice, and land/ 'scape/ memory.
   The Art of Being Human.
Following. *To Create a Universe.*
Nothing Remembers. *The Indian River Review: A Journal of Prose, Poetry, and
   Photog-raphy; The BeZine; Miombo Publishing.*
Return from Pompeii. *Brave Voices Poetry Journal.*
Shackleton. *The World behind it, Chaos.*
Silent Poetry. *Miombo Publishing.*
Sing this at the end. *Some Ride! A Festschrift in Honor of Michael Dennis Browne.*
This ancient place where my footsteps leave no trace. *arc-23.*
Yesterday. The Woven Tale Press; Jerusalism.

The author greatly appreciates the editors of these publications for including these works.

Dust to Dust, Fuzzy logic, That other night when, Up against the wall, and Yesterday appeared first on my blogZine, currently called *Meta/ Phor(e) /Play* (https://MichaelDickel.info).

A few poems may have appeared on Facebook, Instagram, or Twitter, in early drafts.

Two residencies, one with 100 Thousand Poets for Change, in Florida, U.S., and one with HamiltonSeen / Sublimatus, in Ontario, Canada, provided much-needed time and space to work on this book of poems, as well as invaluable creative interaction.

Thanks to Michael Rothenberg for reading this in early form and arguing with me in fun and productive ways until poems in this book became stronger. All errors are my own responsibility.

Michael Dickel's writing and art appear in print and online. His poetry has won international awards and been translated into several languages. Recent books include: a poetry chapbook, *Breakfast at the End of Capitalism*, (2017) and a flash fiction collection, *The Palm Reading after The Toad's Garden* (2016). Previous books include poetry collections: *War Surrounds Us*, and *The World Behind It, Chaos....* He co-edited *Voices Israel Volume 36*, was managing editor for *arc-23* and *arc-24*, and is a past-chair of the Israel Association of Writers in English. He is a contributing editor of *The BeZine* (TheBeZine.com). With Israeli producer / director David Fisher, he received a U.S.A. National Endowment of the Humanities documentary-film development grant through their Bridging Cultures program and wrote a documentary script about Yiddish Theatre.

CPSIA information can be obtained
at www.ICGtesting.com
Printed in the USA
BVHW031517120919
558309BV00001B/280/P